THE COUNTERFEIT
KINGDOM

THE COUNTERFEIT
KINGDOM

A Prophecy to the Modern Church

Larry Dorcik

XULON PRESS

Xulon Press
2301 Lucien Way #415
Maitland, FL 32751
407.339.4217
www.xulonpress.com

Paperback ISBN-13: 978-1-66283-581-0
Ebook ISBN-13: 978-1-66283-582-7

TABLE OF CONTENTS

Acknowledgements vii
Preface ix
Introduction xi

Chapter 1: Of Kings and Kingdoms 1

Chapter 2: The War of the Worlds Intensifies 9

Chapter 3: From Babel to the Anointed 13

Chapter 4: The "Witness" Nation Matures 17

Chapter 5: Daniel's Vision 23

Chapter 6: Constantine I, The "Savior"
of the Church? 33

Chapter 7: The History and Purpose of Conflict 35

Chapter 8: The Age of Conflict to the
Conflict of the Ages 39

Chapter 9: The Millennial Kingdom vs.
The Counterfeit Kingdom 59

Chapter 10: The Book of Revelation 69

Chapter 11: The Challenge 83

Sources 85

ACKNOWLEDGEMENTS

I t is with deepest appreciation and profound gratitude that I acknowledge family and friends who have been a constant source of encouragement and help during this process called writing.

First place must go to the love of my life, Alice Dorcik, for her unwavering support and constant gentle pressure to persevere and complete this work and share it with others.

I also owe an eternal debt of gratitude to the spiritual giants in my life whose teachings and life examples have been the major source of biblical knowledge and revolutionary concepts shared in this book. My first pastor, Harwood Steele of Friendship Baptist Church, introduced me to the importance of Israel in God's great plan of redemption for His creation. To my second pastor, Ken Garrison, of Fellowship Church, I must say your deep scriptural studies and subsequent teachings for thirty-six years laid the foundation for this book.

To my fellow elder, Jon Klein, thank you for bringing your unique Jewish perspective and sense of humor to profound biblical teachings, which enhanced the content of this book. To my current pastor, Roger Diaz of Fellowship Church, thank you for your faithfulness in continuing the ministry started fifty years ago. Your tireless service and unique ability to marry modern geo-political data with biblical prophecy and revelation is far too rare in today's modern church and has played a pivotal role in the content of this writing. Finally, to my brothers and sisters of Fellowship Church, thank you for your prayers and encouragement over the past two years. I am eternally grateful to God for the editorial input from Michael and AnnaMary Lopez and MaryAnne McGrath who were able to "magically" transform my rough manuscript into a beautiful and readable electronic copy suitable for publication.

May God use the work of all our hands to bring light and truth to His church as He establishes His kingdom on the Earth.

PREFACE

"The Kingdom of the World has become The Kingdom of our Lord and of His Messiah; and He will reign forever and ever." Revelation 11:15

This biblical quote is perhaps the most profound and relevant statement for all humanity, especially when one considers the current political and economic condition of today's world. Nations, religions, and even families are experiencing unprecedented polarization. This grand schism, this ideological divide in the human community, screams for light and truth; light and truth which will expose the "Counterfeit Kingdom."

This book is an attempt to help the reader make a clear and concise distinction between the coming kingdom of God and its deceptive counterfeit. Failing to make this distinction will have eternal consequences which will affect the final destiny of myriads of human souls.

INTRODUCTION

In order to gain the greatest benefit from this work, the reader should subscribe to certain fundamental truths:

1. The God of the Bible exists.
2. The Bible is an invaluable source of truth.
3. The Gospels and writings of the Apostles are a natural and critical continuation of the Torah and the prophets.

Even if the reader does not subscribe to the aforementioned "fundamental truths," one may discover a wealth of information, revelation, and hope during this time of tribulation for all of humanity. So "gird up your loins" and "fasten your seat belts," as we race through world history in search of the ever elusive "Counterfeit Kingdom."

CHAPTER 1

OF KINGS AND KINGDOMS

B efore beginning our search for "The Counterfeit Kingdom," we should first gain a deeper understanding of the terms <u>king</u> and <u>kingdom</u>. As citizens of the United States of America, or some other nation not living under a king or queen, the significance of the terms is lost. The significance has been further obscured by the deficiency of historical study in our public and private schools and colleges for the past fifty years. Let's clarify some terminology.

What is a king? A person who has <u>absolute</u> power and authority.

What is a kingdom? In its simplest form, a kingdom is a king's domain. A domain is a land or a people over which a single, sovereign individual (the king) exercises complete authority and control. It is a place where an individual has no rights or authority, unless granted by the king. Failure to obey and submit to the king may result in dire or unpleasant consequences, perhaps even death. Obedience, on the other hand, results in a more pleasant and favorable life. Let's look at some real, modern-day kingdoms.

Great Britain

Great Britain has a queen, but her power has been abdicated to the people through the British Parliament. The queen is not a sovereign ruler in the truest sense. In fact, today, the monarchy may be in the process of dissolving.

Saudi Arabia

The kingdom of Saudi Arabia is much closer to a true kingdom. The king or his princes rule with complete authority and control. There are little to no human rights given to the people. The first two examples are straight forward and easily understood. Let's look at a third kingdom. This next kingdom is much more subtle and may provide some hints to lead us to "The Counterfeit Kingdom," for which we search.

The Magic Kingdom

But wait! How can "The Happiest Place on Earth" be an example of "The Counterfeit Kingdom?" Look carefully at the identifier, The *Magic* Kingdom. Translation: The domain where magic is king. What is magic? Magic is illusion, deception, and control through manipulation. So, let's properly define the "Magic Kingdom." The "Magic Kingdom" is the domain where illusion, deception, and manipulation rule over masses of people from all the nations of the world. Every year, millions from many nations make a pilgrimage to The Magic Kingdom. The pilgrims cannot approach nor enter the kingdom without a gift. The gift is in the form of large amounts of money offered at the gates of the kingdom. In return for the offering, the king promises the people happiness, food, and drink, comfortable housing (for an additional offering of course), and anything else their heart desires. The fourth example is not so visible, and it is not discernable without a dynamic change taking place in the human soul. This change is referred to in the Bible as being "born from above" or "born again." This kingdom is the kingdom of God.

The kingdom of God

Records for the origin of the kingdom of God exist by revelation given to Moses by God Himself. The words, "In the beginning, God created the heavens (the spiritual realm) and the Earth (the physical realm)" (Gen. 1:1) reveal His sovereign power and authority over both realms. So, in the beginning, God was King of both the physical realm and the spiritual realm. The two realms of existence were under one loving, beneficent King who provided everything needed by every living organism in both realms. The King created man to care for and maintain the physical realm. Everything was good and idyllic until...a lying, deceptive agent slithered into the physical realm. This beautiful, but deadly, agent caused a seemingly unbridgeable rift between the two realms. This rift heralded the second Kingdom.

The Kingdom of the World

The Kingdom of the World was birthed through lies, deception, and rebellion. The lies and deception originated from an agent who rebelled against the sovereign authority of the God of Creation and deceived God's servant, man, and changed the world from God-centered to man-centered. This entity is called by various names. Among them are: The

Serpent, The Dragon, the devil, Ha Satan (The Opposer), and the Father of Lies. This evil, lying, rebellious despot illegally took control of God's beautiful creation, and transformed it into a kingdom where the thoughts and actions of all mankind were perpetually evil. Understanding the fundamental nature of this "King of the World," and his kingdom may give us insight and answers to such questions as: Why is there so much evil in the world? Why do so many good people suffer? Why do we have so many devastating wars? Neither the kingdom of God nor the kingdom of the world fully represents "The Counterfeit Kingdom," for which we search. One of them, however, does point to the ancient origins of it, so we must continue the search through the annals of history to discover "The Counterfeit Kingdom." Let's dig a little deeper into the characteristics of these two Kingdoms as revealed through the scriptural timeline. First, we will consider the kingdom of God.

The kingdom of God, in the beginning, was all good. There was nothing evil. There was no death. There was no sickness, no greed, no arrogance, or pride. The relationship between God, man, and creation was pure and perfect. God provided everything needed by man. The earth was the perfect place for mankind to flourish and was a place where God could dwell and interact directly with mankind. God's heavenly creation and His earthly creation together represented His kingdom. He was, and is, a holy, loving compassionate King over both parts of His created domain. The results of this proper relationship were righteousness, peace, and joy in Heaven and earth. These were and are the three primary characteristics of the kingdom of God. But, not for long!

At some point after the creation of the heavenly and earthly realms, there occurred a rebellion in the heavenly realm. Yes, you guessed it! The instigator was none other than the proud, arrogant, lying, and deceiving opponent of everything good...the serpentine dragon himself. Because of his self-serving ambitions to be king of Heaven, he was relieved of his position of power in the heavenly realm, and exiled to the earthly realm, where he began to build himself a kingdom, the kingdom of the world.

The father of lies made his way into Eden, the paradise of God, and thus began the sad saga of the kingdom of the world. Satan presented himself to the unsuspecting caretakers of the world as a benign creature of great beauty. You know the rest of the sordid tale. However, if you don't, read the record in Genesis, chapter 3.

What data can we glean from this ancient record of the kingdom of the world which might help us in the search for "The Counterfeit Kingdom?"

The kingdom of the world was founded on lies and deception designed to redirect man's focus from the God of Creation to a self-serving focus on man. This change in focus opened a channel of spiritual communication with the one who would be king of the world, Satan himself. The results of this heretofore unknown communication process were catastrophic! Immediately, man experienced fear and shame when confronted by the King, the God of Creation. Mankind's relationship with God was shattered and they were forced out of His holy presence by satanic deception, and their own disobedience and rebellion. The catastrophes piled up:

- Death became a real and fearsome prospect.
- Man had to provide for himself because the new king of the world could not, and the God of Creation could not allow the continuing cooperation of the earth.
- Murder was committed in the first family, as Cain killed his brother, Able. (Genesis 4:8)
- Evil activities ran rampant on the earth.
- The kingdom of God was no longer a visible kingdom on earth, as He withdrew His visible presence.

By now, the differences between the kingdom of God and the kingdom of the world should be clear and obvious. If it is still a little foggy, go back and reread the narrative presented herein and compare it to the narrative of Scripture. In the meantime, we press on in our search for "The Counterfeit Kingdom."

CHAPTER 2

THE WAR OF THE WORLDS INTENSIFIES

The conditions in the kingdom of the world became so unbearably evil that God decided to destroy all living things on earth. Then, as He arrived at this unthinkable decision, He discovered a minute remnant of the kingdom of God...Noah and his family. We all know the childhood story of Noah, the ark, and the flood. If you have never heard this fascinating story, read about it in your Bible or take a family trip to Kentucky, The Blue Grass State, check out, and tour the impressive full-scale reproduction of the ark.

Let's take a more mature view of what is really taking place in this ancient narrative. It's not about cute animals and an awesome family of carpenters building a gigantic ship. The biblical record shows the grace and mercy of an omnipotent King providing a bridge to salvation for all living things on earth. Even more profound is the concept of the continuation of the kingdom of God on earth. Without this righteous family and their faith in and obedience to the Word God gave them concerning the ark and the flood, there would have been nothing left on earth to manifest the beauty and glory of God or His kingdom. If you peer intently into the future, you may even glimpse another righteous family of carpenters who were instrumental in an even more profound salvation process.

Another often-overlooked concept in the account of Noah and the flood is the limiting effect on the ability of the evil Dragon king of this world to carry out his nefarious plans. Because of the long lifespan of man and the interactions with the spirit realm prior to the flood, each man could do evil things for a thousand years or more. God, in His infinite wisdom, removed evil from the earth through the flood and further limited the potential for evil by limiting the lifespan of man. Instead of living for a thousand years or more, man's lifespan was reduced by a factor of ten, and even today it remains at plus or minus one hundred years.

Although it may appear that our quest for "The Counterfeit Kingdom" may have wandered into the weeds of history, "do not doubt me," (as Rush Limbaugh often said) we're still on track, like a good bloodhound on the hunt for an escaped evildoer.

Noah's sons, Shem, Ham and Japheth, became the progenitors of all the nations of the world. The king of the world began to work his evil magic and deception again. Under his leadership, mankind was unified by one language and soon began to be used by the king of the world to attempt to conquer the kingdom of God. The plan was to build some sort of mechanism, "a tower," to reconnect the physical and spiritual realms, thereby bringing both under the control of the unrelenting king of the world. Apparently, there was a strong possibility of success because God again intervened. He thwarted the efforts of the king of the world by striking and destroying the powerful spirit of unity in the people. This masterful stroke destroyed the ability of men to communicate by confusing the common language. This inability to communicate ultimately caused the dispersion of mankind throughout the earth. This is only the beginning of the Babel saga. Behold! I think we may have discovered the first clue in our search for "The Counterfeit Kingdom." "The Counterfeit Kingdom" requires **unity** and **communication**. Hold this clue in your mind as we continue our search.

At this point in world history, other extra-biblical records become available to help us understand the development of the kingdom of the world. Written records began to be widely used in the cradles of civilization. Hieroglyphs in Egypt and cuneiform symbols in the Euphrates River Valley recorded business transactions, lifestyles, exploits of men, and forms of religious activities, just as the early Hebrew writings do. Many good books have already been written and commentaries created about these subjects. If you wish to gain additional knowledge of these subjects, feel free to do so. But remember, our search is not only about gaining additional knowledge. Our quest is to uncover "The Counterfeit Kingdom." We must keep a laser sharp focus as we search through millennia of history to discover this elusive domain and clearly discern its purpose. But wait! Back up to the start of the paragraph... business...lifestyle...exploits of men... forms of religious activities? We almost passed our second clue! This "Counterfeit Kingdom" is all about **man and his self-centered existence.** These attributes are also common to the kingdom of the world. We still have not yet discovered enough clues to clearly identify our objective. Let's continue our wandering through the murky annals of time to filter out a few more clues.

CHAPTER 3

FROM BABEL TO THE ANOINTED

From the northern reaches of the ancient "Fertile Crescent," a rather remarkable character emerged from the mists of time. This man was chosen, by the God of Creation, for a most formidable task. Avram was called to father a nation which would be an example to all the nations, a proof, a witness of the value of living in the kingdom of God rather than the kingdom of the world (Genesis 12:1-3). It was a nation to begin to assist with the restoration, dare we say redemption, of all that was lost when man was removed from the garden. It was to be a nation which gladly submitted itself to the God of Creation; a nation in which the King could take up residence and renew the intimacy between the creator and His creation.

The hope for the restoration of this relationship got off to a rather rocky start because, guess who, the opposer, began to prey upon the human vulnerabilities of Avram. Avram was given a new name, Avraham, and an <u>eternal</u> covenant with the God of Creation. This covenant was reaffirmed to his promised son, Isaac, and his grandson, Jacob.

Jacob, through twenty-one years of difficulties, finally embraced his appointed destiny. There in the ancient valley of the Jordan, near the confluence of the Jabbok, Jacob was transformed! So great was the transformation, he was given a new name: <u>Israel!</u>

Israel's twelve sons became the nucleus of the nation yet to be born. The birth of the nation of Israel would take 400 years (and you thought nine months was tough). The record of the gestation period of this developing nation is found in the books of Genesis and Exodus. If you want more of the pregnant details, it is a fascinating read. Details about Joseph, Pharaoh, the sons of Israel, and life in the womb of Egypt await those with inquiring minds.

Not to belabor the analogy, but there is one more important character to introduce: the midwife. He is an Egyptian Hebrew named Moses. Yes, he is the very same man through whom God provides the written record we have followed in this narrative.

Allow me to reintroduce another more sinister and all too familiar character, none other than the king of the world. As always, he's lurking in the shadows of time, waiting for an opportunity to wreak havoc. This time Ha Satan is like a lion crouching at the birthing stool, as the midwife (Moses) assists with the delivery. The beast waits to consume the infant nation. As in all childbirth, the arrival of the newborn is preceded by unbearable waves of pain. The pain is brought on by the ten terrible plagues put on Egypt by the God of Creation. As in all births, blood was copious as tens of thousands of substitute Passover lambs were slain to complete the birth. Having failed to consume the infant nation at birth, the great Satan, through his unwitting servants in the house of Pharaoh, would make yet another attempt to eliminate the newborn nation. Again, the God of Creation demonstrated His awesome power and complete authority over the king of the world by crushing the Egyptian army in the waters of the sea (Exodus 1-15).

The delivery was complete. As in all new births, the sound of joyous celebration reverberated across the southern Sinai Desert. The nation of Israel was born and destined to become the greatest nation among all the nations of the kingdom of the world.

CHAPTER 4

THE "WITNESS" NATION MATURES

J oin me as we take a little time to search through the family album of this favored child nation. We will take a quick look at "photos" of the growth and development of Israel as she matures amid the quirky, often dangerous family of nations under the influence of the kingdom of the world.

Early "photos" feature family members like Moses, Aaron, and Joshua. We will see very familiar family characteristics in descendants like David, Samuel, and Jesus of Nazareth. We will also see "photos" of black sheep members of the family, like King Saul. Some of these characteristics may provide clues in our search. So, let's look at some old family photos.

What characteristics do we see in Moses which are indicative of a man functioning in the kingdom of God rather than the kingdom of the world, or "The Counterfeit Kingdom" for which we search?

- Moses, like Abraham, <u>encountered God.</u>
- Moses was <u>obedient.</u>
- Moses was a <u>servant</u> to God and His people, Israel.
- Moses was <u>instrumental</u> in delivering this newborn nation from bondage in a foreign land to a position of maturity in the land which God had promised.

Let's turn a page in the album and look at a shepherd turned king: David, the son of Jessie.

- David, like Moses and Abraham, <u>encountered God</u> early in his life, as a shepherd in his father's pastures in Judea.
- David was <u>obedient</u> to the call given him by God through the prophet Samuel.
- David, as king, <u>served</u> God and Israel.
- King David was <u>instrumental</u> in bringing the young nation of Israel to full maturity.

Flip another page and see images of Jesus of Nazareth, a Man who encountered God, and is an eternal part of the Creator of Heaven and Earth.

- Jesus, like His forefathers, <u>encountered God</u>, but on a more constant and intimate level.
- Jesus was <u>obedient,</u> even to the point of death.
- Jesus was a <u>servant</u> to Israel, as He ministered through teaching, healing, and deliverance. His ministry to the nations continues through His body, the church, and the nation of Israel to our present day.
- Jesus was and is <u>instrumental</u> in God's purpose by reconciling all mankind to the God of Abraham, Isaac, and Jacob. To put it another way, he provided a way for all mankind to recapture the intimate relationship, which was lost when men chose a self-centered, rather than a God-centered, life.

There is one final and critical image of Jesus to be indelibly etched into our memory. Like the midwife, Moses, Jesus was responsible for the birth of a witness, the "Second Witness"—the church. The church was at that time, and should be today, a living organism to continue to demonstrate, before all men, four powerful concepts of the kingdom of God. The first concept deals with how to develop a relationship with the God of Creation. The second concept reveals the value of obedience to Him. The third is service to God, Israel, and mankind. The fourth concept is to be instrumental in re-establishing the kingdom of God <u>on</u> Earth! This "Second Witness" would be a living structure to house the presence of God on the Earth. Now, let's look at the "black sheep" we mentioned earlier.

There have been an amazing number of rulers of Israel who are good examples of being a "black sheep." For the sake of moving on in our search, we'll look at a snapshot of Saul, the first king of Israel. Saul was a national leader chosen for all the <u>wrong</u> reasons.

Saul became king by popular demand of the people of Israel. The people wanted to be like all the other nations, with a good-looking, strong king of whom they could be proud. The historically rebellious people of Israel rejected the power and authority of an <u>unseen</u> God. Their preference was to be like all the nations around them rather than an example, a <u>witness</u>, of a righteous and holy way of life which was required by this often-obscured deity.

As we view Saul's life through the lens of Scripture, we see a tall, handsome man totally devoid of spiritual anointing. Saul was a man with strong tendencies to focus on himself and turn to the dark side of spirituality for strength. Take special note of these four characteristics:

1. Looks good.
2. An improper response to his godly anointing.
3. Self-focused.
4. The tendency to turn to the king of the world.

Hmmm...could we have another clue to "The Counterfeit Kingdom?" So, what can we conclude from these "snapshots?" Totally unlike the preceding characters, Saul:

- <u>Did have a real encounter</u> with God and was anointed by Samuel, though he was unable to fulfill the requirements of that anointing.
- <u>Was not obedient</u> to the God of Israel.
- <u>Served his own interests</u> rather than the kingdom of God or the people of Israel.
- <u>Was not instrumental</u> in encouraging the people of Israel to be a good witness of the kingdom of God before other nations.

We could review many more biblical records of men like the kings of Israel and the high priesthood of the first century A.D. It seems a bit redundant though, since they exhibited many of the same characteristics of King Saul. So, let's close the family album for now and push our search forward in time.

From the first century A.D. to the present, history is recorded by an ever-expanding cadre of record-keepers. This plethora of historical data can be very enlightening but can also obscure the clues pertinent to our search for "The Counterfeit Kingdom."

CHAPTER 5

DANIEL'S VISION

C ome with me now for a whirlwind tour of the great kingdoms of the world. We'll need to backtrack briefly before being catapulted forward a couple of millennia. We will use a rather unique approach for this tour. The prophet Daniel reveals an incredibly concise picture of the kingdoms of the world from about 600 B.C. to modern times.

Envision, if you will, a magnificent, giant statue of a man, not at all like modern statues of bronze or marble. This awesome statue had a head of pure gold. Its chest and arms were of silver. Its abdomen and thighs were of fine bronze. The legs were iron, and the feet were a mixture of iron and clay pottery.

Daniel described the statue as representing kingdoms of the world from the perspective of the God of Creation. The head of gold was so valuable because it represented a kingdom with absolute authority. It was very similar to the structure of the kingdom of God; and therefore, had great value in God's economy.

Daniel clearly identified this kingdom as the Kingdom of Babylon.

The next portion of the statue's anatomy was made of pure silver. As we all know, silver is valuable but less valuable than gold. Therefore, if we continue the kingdom analogy, this next world kingdom is less like the Kingdom of Babylon and less representative of the kingdom of God. The silver portion of the statue represents the Medo-Persian kingdom. It consisted of two kingdoms joining forces to overthrow a kingdom of singular authority. The known world was now under the weaker, less valuable, authority of two rulers. This Medo-Persian kingdom was sustained for about 200 years. Then, the Greeks arrived!

The kingdom of Greece gained control of the known world around 300 years before the time of Jesus. From God's perspective, this bronze kingdom was even less valuable as a governmental structure. It was far removed from His original gold standard. Its fundamental flaw was the concept of authority invested in the people rather than absolute authority in one king as in Babylon or two kings, as in the Medo-Persian kingdom.

Following the untimely death of Alexander, the Great, the authority of the Greek kingdom was further diluted through the establishment of four rulers of the known world. These four rulers were ultimately consumed by the overwhelming power of Rome (the legs of Iron).

Things don't get much better in the kingdom of the world after the Romans wrestled control of the world from the Greeks. The Roman Empire built upon the foundation of the Greek governmental structure, and the philosophical musings of highly educated men. They were masters of manipulation of the people over whom they exercised authority. Their legendary ruthlessness and depravity struck fear in the hearts of all the nations.

It was in the midst of this chaos that the God of Creation inserted His Anointed One and laid the visible foundation for the re-establishment of the kingdom of God on the Earth. That foundation consisted of Jesus (The Cornerstone) and His twelve faithful, spirit-filled disciples (the foundation stones). The structure which would be built on that foundation would be unlike anything ever seen in the kingdom of the world. In fact, it would ultimately replace the kingdom of the world. But how?

The lowest level of the great statue was the feet of clay and iron. The clay (ceramic) comes from earth and represents, from God's viewpoint, a governmental structure (kingdom) of the lowest quality. It is also the weakest since it is based on the authority of the masses of people on the earth. To further demonstrate the weakness of this final level of worldly governments, fragments of iron (remnants of the Roman legs of iron) were mixed with the ceramic. This fragile mixture of opposing elements leaves the great statue vulnerable to total destruction.

Daniel's final revelation revealed how the great statue, the kingdom of the world, was laid low. God used a tool, a stone, to crush the fragile feet and bring down all forms of earthly government. This single stone would expand to become a great mountain and cover the whole earth. This analogy represents a kingdom of great power, a kingdom which would govern the whole earth with law and righteousness. This kingdom would <u>never</u> be replaced...the kingdom of God. This kingdom of which Daniel spoke was indeed the kingdom revealed by God's Anointed One, Jesus of Nazareth.

The unseen foundation of the kingdom of God was poured when the God of Creation, by His dynamic Word, spoke everything into existence. As we discussed earlier, God was sovereign over all His Creation, both spiritual and physical. The true structure of the kingdom of God was not clearly discernible until the Anointed One, Jesus, appeared on the world scene.

Jesus, in His thirty-plus years on planet Earth, brought all mankind three astonishing, revelatory concepts. First, He revealed the most concise descriptions of the nature and purposes of the kingdom of God.

Recorded in the gospels, one can find Jesus's "Sermon on the Mount," and the many parables given to His early disciples, provide a clearer understanding of the kingdom of God. Jesus clearly stated that His primary, God-given purpose was to preach (declare) the good news of the coming kingdom of God. That message was fundamental in His early years of ministry in Israel. Even more significant was the reality that He and His disciples demonstrated the power and authority of the God of Creation over the god of this world kingdom through miracles of healing, provision, and deliverance.

The second concept of demonstrating God-given power and authority amid God's first witness (Israel) was revealed to give the nations a clearer view of what life could be like under the kingship of the God of Creation.

The third concept revealed was the construction of a pathway, a very narrow pathway back to the Garden of Eden, to a time of reunion between all men and the Creator. The cost of that construction project was unimaginably exorbitant. It was a cost borne solely by a God who loved His creation so much that His own Son's physical life was taken to pay the total cost. The very source of Jesus's physical life, His blood, paved that narrow pathway back to God for every human who longs for life in the presence of the God of Creation.

Let's take a moment to re-orient ourselves. Remember, we are searching for "The Counterfeit Kingdom." To identify a counterfeit, it is helpful to first clearly discern what is being imitated. To this point, we've scoured the pages of ancient history and two adversarial kingdoms have been revealed. The kingdom of God and the kingdom of the world should now be much more clearly discernible. In order to gain an even clearer view and discover more clues to "The Counterfeit Kingdom," we will take advantage of the ever-expanding written records of the more recent past. We will explore the growth of the kingdom of the world and follow the sometimes barely discernible track of the kingdom of

God. Perhaps we may discover more clues to the identity of the third kingdom. This third, subtle and devious kingdom becomes a broad road to eternal destruction for all who are careless enough to follow it.

The Roman Empire exhibited one of the fundamental characteristics of "The Counterfeit Kingdom," opposition to God's two witnesses. The Roman Empire, the pre-emanate kingdom of the world during and after the time of Jesus, had quite a record of opposition to Israel and the Church. This opposition was so intense that it began to seem like tribulation, as described by Jesus.

Around 70 A.D., the Romans sacked Jerusalem and dispersed virtually all the remaining nation of Israel into every corner of the civilized world. The king of this world seemed to have succeeded in destroying the first witness. He would release the full force of his surrogates in Rome against the second witness, the newborn Church. Horrible persecution of the Church was well documented and continued over 200 years. You know the horrendous stories of Christians, wild beasts, Roman coliseums, and death by crucifixion. As if all that was not enough trouble, the opposer began to drive a wedge between the two witnesses.

The religious leaders of the first and second century church, under the influence of politics and philosophy, began to inexorably drift away from the formerly close relationship with Israel and the foundational truths of Torah and the prophets. The ever-widening gulf between Israel and the Church did not bode well for the expression of the kingdom of God in the earth for the next 2000 years. The primary character responsible for this sad state of affairs was Constantine I, Emperor of the Roman Empire.

Emperor Constantine I is definitely a person of interest who requires deeper scrutiny. The record of history has some fascinating and enlightening revelations about this man who aspired to be a god.

CHAPTER 6

CONSTANTINE I, THE "SAVIOR" OF THE CHURCH?

As Constantine I ascended to prominence in the Roman world, this great iron kingdom was beginning to descend, as do all kingdoms of the world. The effort to maintain control over the vast kingdom was taking its toll on the government in Rome. The demands of far-flung wars and the disenfranchised masses were exceeding the government's ability to supply. After a reported battlefield epiphany, Constantine I offered a solution.

His solution involved what amounted to an alliance between the representatives of the kingdom of the world and the representatives of the kingdom of God. He, Constantine I, represented the power and authority of the Roman empire, and the Church represented the power and authority of God. It was a match made in... well... *not* Heaven. The unholy offspring of this union became known as "The Holy Roman Empire."

This unholy union previews the tumultuous relationship between the church and world governments which continues today. The blow-by-blow accounts of this tragedy are recorded very well by a long list of world and church historians and are beyond the scope of this work. For our purposes, in our search for the elusive "Counterfeit Kingdom," it is enough to see the conflict. Whoa! Conflict? A clue? Yes, "The Counterfeit Kingdom" arises through **conflict.**

CHAPTER 7

THE HISTORY AND PURPOSE OF CONFLICT

Since conflict is such an important clue, let's explore a while. Initially, we will look at conflict in God's two earthly witnesses to all the nations. (Later, we will explore conflict in the nations.) The two witnesses, of course, are the nation of Israel and the church of Jesus, the Anointed One.

First, let's look at an update on the condition of God's first witness. After the dispersion process, Assyrian in 732 B.C., Babylonian in 586 B.C., and finally the Roman in 70 A.D., the power of unity in Israel was neutralized, just like the unity of the nations at Babel. The spiritual power of unity in Israel was further bound by the development of various sects of what is known as Judaism. The "Echad" (oneness) could no longer be demonstrated to the nations. The power and authority of God was hidden from the nations by the cloak of conflict within the diaspora.

The second witness did not fare any better. God's second witness, the church, began to lose its unity and spiritual power within the first century of its founding. The very opposite of the thing for which Jesus prayed in John 17 began to occur. The church fathers began to embrace the ways of the world. They began to rely on human philosophy and intellectual reasoning rather than power and wisdom from On High. The church split into east and west branches then shattered into a multitude of discordant and often deadly shards.

Just like the first witness, the second witness's spiritual power was hidden from the nations by the darkness of conflict and remained hidden until the 16th century when the church began to seek reformation.

Don't despair, there is a silver lining in this cloud of gloom. Through all this conflict in God's two witnesses, there remained a nearly invisible thread of righteousness. There always existed a faithful remnant in Israel who followed the Torah, and a remnant in the church who faithfully followed the teachings of Jesus. The two witnesses would, in fact, be brought to prominence in the world three centuries later through the rebirth of the nation of Israel and the concurrent revival within the church.

So, what could be the true purpose for all this conflict in God's two witnesses? In dispersed Israel, there grew a deep desire and longing for a return to the promises and blessings seen in Torah, a return to the unity of a homeland and the God of their Fathers. The church began to long for a return to the righteousness, peace, joy, and unity of the first century church. This long age of conflict created a deep desire for the spiritual life and power demonstrated by Jesus. This period of conflict served to bring God's two witnesses back to a position of empowerment to serve God and the nations in the final stages of the redemption of all creation.

Let's take a short break and look in the upper right section of your brain for the "searching cart" icon. Click on that icon to review the clues. After this break, we will return to our search.

- Clue #1 – Unity and Communication.
- Clue #2 – Self-Orientation.
- Clue #3 – Opposition to God.
- Clue #4 – Conflict.

CHAPTER 8

THE AGE OF CONFLICT TO THE CONFLICT OF THE AGES

R emember, we are scouring the pages of biblical and secular history for clues which will lead us to "The Counterfeit Kingdom." The first three clues led us to the fourth. Perhaps the fourth will lead to more or maybe it is the final clue?

Let's pick up the thread we left before the brief memory exercise. We will broaden our perspective to include the expanding conflict in the nations.

As the reformation period of the church was beginning in Europe, the discovery of The New World of North and South America heralded a whole new age of conflict on a global scale. At the same time, God's two witnesses began to awaken from 1500 years of slumber.

The nations of the world, particularly Spain, England, France, the Netherlands, and Portugal, began to battle for control of the vast treasures and resources of these two new continents. World commerce in gold, silver, and exotic consumables exploded. The nations of Europe laid claim to these treasures, supposedly under the authority of the church or the authority of the king. The result of these self-focused actions was... you guessed it: conflict. The primary forces driving this global conflict were The Industrial Age and the vast fortunes to be made.

This new industrial age brought almost unbelievable technological advances and dramatic social and economic changes. The feudal kingdoms of Europe were rapidly being replaced by wealthy, powerful leaders in business, manufacturing and world trade. The growth of this fledgling world economy was mind-boggling.

The horse and wagon were made obsolete by gasoline-powered automobiles and trucks. Massive and powerful steamships, powered by coal, circumnavigated the globe much more quickly than the graceful, tall-masted sailing ships driven by prevailing winds. Huge quantities of raw materials like iron ore, coal and timber were transported by new railroads crisscrossing the Americas, Europe, Africa and the far east. In just a couple of centuries, the kingdom of the world experienced an unprecedented revolution, and the revolution would lead to a very sinister and deadly turn of events.

In order to more fully understand the nature of this "turn of events," we will attempt to set the world stage by reviewing the nature and condition of the world in the 18th and 19th centuries. During this period of momentous change, the kingdom of the world, the kingdom of God, and "The Counterfeit Kingdom" are moving forward in time on parallel paths, sometimes crossing, and sometimes clashing. The kingdom of the world is more visible. The kingdom of God is less visible but becoming more so due to the reformation movement in the church and a new hope in dispersed Israel. "The Counterfeit Kingdom" is still hidden behind the clouds and dust raised by seemingly endless conflict and the raging expansion of world commerce.

Painful though it may be, it is important to review some statistics which reflect the character of the kingdom of the world, and thereby its king, Satan. Conflict seems to be the overarching characteristic of the kingdom of the world, and the pain comes from the results of the conflict. (The cost, in terms of human life and world-wide economics, pours the foundation of "The Counterfeit Kingdom.")

This seems to be an opportune time to audit the cost. Although the cost of global conflict spreads the pain, a narrow audit of America's conflicts should suffice to make the point. Let's look at the cost of The American Revolutionary War and then The American Civil War.

The American Revolutionary War (1775 -1783) birthed a new nation in the global family of nations. This constitutional republic was founded on Judeo-Christian principles, and it would mature into the most powerful and wealthy nation in the world, but the cost would be high. As in all births, there would be blood.

- Human Lives: +/- 40,000
- Financial Cost: Britain, 250 million pounds
- France: 1.3 billion livres
- Spain: 700 million reales
- USA: 400 million dollars in wages alone

The American Civil War (1861 -1865) was brought about by discontent with the economic system based on slavery and the political control of that system. Another factor involved disputes about states' rights. The southern, less industrialized states, pushed for state control independent of a centralized federal government. The northern, industrialized and wealthier states preferred the centralized federal government, which would exercise control over individual states. The result of this conflict was a devastating war which raged for four long years.

- Human Lives: 620,000
- Financial Cost: 15.5 billion dollars

Another clue? Control? Yes, **political and economic control.** "The counterfeit kingdom is all about control. The subtle, insidious nature of "The Counterfeit Kingdom" is about to make its debut. The opening curtains of the world stage take place in the theatre of war.

- Act One: World War I

The scene opens in Europe at the dawn of the 20th century. The leading actors are:

- Lenin of Russia
- Wilhelm of Germany
- Clemenceau of France
- Asquith of England
- Wilson of the United States of America

There are also many other supporting actors from the nations.

"As it was in the days of Noah..." These words spoken by Jesus, the Anointed One, resonate throughout the grand theatre. The stage erupts with the sounds of gunfire and deafening artillery explosions. The atmosphere is polluted by the acrid smell of burnt gunpowder and the deadly, choking fog of poisonous mustard gas. The screams of the wounded and the silence of the dead bear witness to a new age of conflict.

Almost the whole world is at war, the west and the east battle for control of this new world of industry and wealth. As the curtain falls on Act One, the battle for the soul of mankind begins.

- Human Lives: 40 million
- Financial Cost: 208 billion dollars

Act II will begin after a brief intermission.

The king of the world has battled for control of all the souls of mankind since the tragic garden incident. When he succeeds to gain control of a human soul, that soul becomes a physical manifestation of his attributes in the world.

To gain control, the deceiver must "trap" each soul. Like any good trapper, Satan must set a trap and use an enticing bait. The trap is the fallen, self-focused mind of all man. The bait is satanic communication with the mind.

The human mind is incredibly vulnerable to spiritual communication from the great liar, just as it was in the garden at the beginning. The human soul (the eternal component of all men) is tasked with the difficult work of filtering the constant flow of information received and processed by the mind. This process of filtration involves choosing what is right or wrong relative to self or relative to God. Choices made by the soul, either set the trap or disable it. If the soul decides relative to self, the trap is set. If the soul decides relative to God, the trap is disabled. If the trap is set, the only thing needed to complete the capture is...the bait.

The favorite and most effective "bait" used by the opposer is a lie. If the soul chooses to believe the lie (take the bait), the satanic trap is sprung, and the soul is captured. This captured soul begins to manifest the characteristics of Satan himself and becomes a slave to the lying accuser. The enslaved soul must endure condemnation, false accusations, evil thoughts, and actions which continue unabated unless a godly intervention brings deliverance. The depths of this enslavement will become more obvious as we continue with Act II.

World War II

The year is 1848 A.D. As the curtain opens for Act II, Scene I begins with two characters seemingly unrelated, but central to the theme of conflict: one now infamous Karl Marx and his cohort Fredrick Engles. These two characters begin to build on the foundation of "The Counterfeit Kingdom" (the pouring of the foundation was announced a few pages back). Both are working intently on a document which will profoundly impact the trajectory of the kingdom of this world. The lights fade to black in anticipation of Scene 2.

The year is 1939. Scene 2 opens with a whole new cast of characters:

- Stalin of Russia
- Hitler of Germany
- De Gaulle of France
- Churchill of England
- F.D. Roosevelt of the USA
- Mussolini of Italy
- Hirohito of Japan

The conflict in the kingdom of the world now spans the whole earth. The deadly capabilities of the machinery of war have taken a quantum leap forward thanks to the unfettered growth of industry and science. Add to the mix an insatiable appetite for power in world leaders under the ruthless control of Satan, and you have a recipe for conflict of grotesque proportions.

The ancient land masses of Europe and Africa are stained by the blood of millions of fighters and innocents. The oceans of the world opened to receive the remains of tens of thousands of brave seamen and airmen. The grisly scene ends abruptly in the blinding flash of nuclear fission. As giant mushroom clouds rise over the Land of the Rising Sun, the actors pause, as if a sudden awareness of self-destruction and the futility of war has flooded their souls. It's only a pause. The king of the world is unrepentant and still in control.

85 million dead and 4.1 trillion (in today's dollars) spent.

We could remain in this theatre for Acts 3, 4, and 5, but it seems unnecessary to see scenes from Korea, Vietnam, and Desert Storm. By now, it seems obvious that conflict in the kingdom of the world is a key element in the emergence of "The Counterfeit Kingdom."

Where is the kingdom of God amid this raging conflict on Earth? Perhaps the description given by Jesus is most apropos: "The kingdom of God is within you." For the people of faith, the church and Israel, the kingdom was internal. For 1500 years, the kingdom of God within the church was overshadowed by the Roman Catholic Church or "universal church." For the dispersed nation of Israel, Judaism both covered and preserved the kingdom of God within them. Though the kingdom of God was not a "shining city," it was a faint glow on the horizon of time and would soon be revealed.

The church re-emerged through what history refers to as three great awakenings. The first (1730-1740) was like a wave of spiritual enthusiasm, particularly in the American colonies. The second (1800-1830s), focused on personal salvation and began the restoration movement. The third (1857-modern times) spread worldwide and heralded Pentecostalism and the charismatic movement. From Azusa Street in 1907 through the 1970s, the church began to search for ways to recapture and exercise the spiritual power and authority so evident in the church of the first century A.D. As the church blossomed, there developed an amazing nexus with the reborn nation of Israel.

Israel, in diaspora, began to come to life in the 1800s, just as the church did. It seems there is more than coincidence here. The two witnesses of the kingdom of God were being propelled into world prominence at the same time. Their paths were still parallel but were beginning to move toward a point of intersection and unity.

The modern Zionist movement began, in earnest, in the 1800s through leaders like Herzl, Weizmann, Balfour, and Ben-Gurion. These early champions of Israel's return to the land of their fathers were often encouraged by Christians. William Hechler was a great encourager of Theodor Herzl. Many other Christians who supported the restoration of Zion preceded and followed Hechler. Men like Edward Cazalet, Lawrence Oliphant, and William E. Blackstone.

The restoration of dispersed Israel began as a trickle in the 16th and 17th centuries, then a steady flow in the 18th and 19th centuries, and finally a flood in the 20th century. In the 1940s, as the horrors of Nazi Germany were revealed to the world community, the path to Zion was opened. The words of the biblical prophets came to life as a nation which had been seen as dead for two thousand years, began to be restored.

The faint glow from the kingdom of God slashed through the darkened world like the rays of the morning sun. The church came alive as the great tent revivals gave way to stadiums filled with tens of thousands of hungry souls searching for new spiritual life. Great evangelists like Billy Graham used the new technologies of radio and television to infuse new life and hope in the people of the nations.

At virtually the same time, the nation of Israel was reborn. In 1948, God's witness nation was re-established in the land of her forefathers. Hatikvah (The Hope) became the call to return for the sons and daughters of Jacob. Just as the prophets declared, the waste places were rebuilt, and the desert burst into bloom.

God's two witnesses were alive and functioning. The kingdom of God was becoming visible again. It sounded too good to be true... and it was! The seeds of the counterfeit kingdom, sown in the 1800s, begin to sprout like tares in God's grand wheat field. Nothing can be done until the fields are harvested. Even God's two witnesses will be deeply affected by this evil sowing.

Before we explore the depths of this "evil sowing," let's review our clues in the search for this counterfeit kingdom:

- Clue #1 - Unity and communication
- Clue #2 - Self-orientation
- Clue #3 - Opposition to God
- Clue #4 - Conflict

There is, I believe, at least one more clue. Ancient governments used their power to control the major civilizations and conquer the world of their day. We've seen hints earlier in this work. Let's take a deep dive into the more modern history of the world and try to recover a few pearls of wisdom.

Following the conflict of WWI, the leaders of the nations launched an effort to re-establish unity through communication which was lost at Babel. History records the effort as "The League of Nations." Communication technologies became the prime facilitator for rapid international relationships. Telephones already replaced telegraphs and the transatlantic telephone cable became the umbilical cord providing a life support system for the league of nations.

The League of Nations became the platform from which the United Nations was launched following the global conflict of WWII. The United Nations was touted as the organization which would lead the world into a new era of peace, health and prosperity. The reality seems to be that The United Nations was hijacked by the "New World Order."

The public announcement was made in June 1992 at the United Nations "Conference on Environment and Development" in Rio De Janeiro, Brazil. The declaration was made by none other than the president of the lone superpower, "King George (Bush) I."

His announcement introduced a document outlining the objectives and methodology to establish a "New World Order." This document, Agenda 21, is a blueprint for restructuring the existing world order in the 21st century. Although the objectives of Agenda 21 are cloaked in terminology like "human rights" and "environmental protection," the real objective (just like "The Counterfeit Kingdom") is political and economic control of the world.

Gaining this level of control demands ongoing global conflict and instability. The existing order in the world must be broken down by any means possible in order to establish the "new" order. Perhaps this "new" world order is not all that new. Remember the Garden of Eden incident?

Rather than overt global warfare like World War I and II, global conflict has taken on new and more subtle manifestations. The multifaceted nature of modern conflict is designed to generate fear within the populations of the world community. Pandemic fear in the people of all nations brings unbearable political and economic pressure to bear on all forms of government. This extreme pressure forces the people of the nations to demand someone or something to alleviate the fear pressure and restore order and peace.

In order to affirm the postulations of the previous paragraphs, let's do a quick review of more recent world history, which promotes fear in the world.

1914 - World War I

1919 - Spanish Flu

1929 - 1930 - The Great Depression

1940s and 1950s - Fear of Nuclear Annihilation like Hiroshima and Nagasaki, Japan.
    - Polio Epidemic

1950s and 1960s - The Cold War between the USA & USSR
- Asian Flu Pandemic
- Korean War
- Cuban Missile Crisis

1970s and 1980s - Social Upheaval
- Rampant drug abuse
- Abortion (population control)
- Threat of new Ice Age

1990s and 2000 - Global Warming
- Deforestation
- Ongoing middle east conflict
- "Desert Storm"

2000 to 2021 - Arab Spring
- Never ending middle east conflict
- H1N1 Pandemic
- Immigration Issues
- Attempted coup against President Trump
- Corona/Covid 19 Pandemic
- Social upheaval
- Defunding police

Do you see the new clue? Yes, **fear** is a key building block for "The Counterfeit Kingdom." The aforementioned sources of fear serve as a catalyst to accelerate the development of the "New World Order." The New World Order is simply the most recent manifestation of the kingdom of the world, and "The Counterfeit Kingdom" is the mechanism by which this new order is being established.

Maybe now is a good time to review our clues, the very hallmarks of this "Counterfeit Kingdom."

1. Unity and communication
2. Self-orientation
3. Opposition to God
4. Conflict
5. Political and economic control
6. Fear

As we have been searching for "The Counterfeit Kingdom," current events have exposed it for all to see. The whole world has experienced political, social, environmental, economic, and religious upheaval. What is being seen today is the culmination of more than two centuries of man's best efforts to bring order to a world spiraling toward destruction. The methodology employed is clearly visible if one carefully considers the six clues and makes a quick review of world history. I think we are very close to identifying this "Counterfeit Kingdom." We will begin our review of "The Counterfeit Kingdom's founding in the 3rd Century BC.

The Mauryan Empire of India has been described by some as "a socialized monarchy," and "a sort of state socialism." Aristophanes produced a Greek play described as socialist and feminist. The character Praxagora put it this way, "I shall begin by making land, money, everything that is private property, common to all." In the 6th century A.D., the Persian priest Mazdak instituted a religion-based socialist system. But things really got rolling in 1789 during the French Revolution. By 1848, "scientific socialism" swept Europe and soon after spread to Australia, thanks to the writings of Karl Marx and Friedrich Engels.

By 1968, the new "left" in America began to adopt causes like environmentalism, feminism, and progressivism. Now, in the 21st century, Venezuelan President Hugo Chavez implemented policies nationalizing national assets like oil. Many other Latin American countries are following suit.

We haven't even begun to address China, Russia, and Indonesia. Perhaps, for the sake of moving forward, allow me to recommend a personal, in-depth search of the history of socialism.

Yes, my faithful reader, "The Counterfeit Kingdom" is the modern-day, radical socialist movement. It's ultimate goal of world control is marketed to the world under the more palatable term, "The New World Order." As you have seen during our brief visits through world history, this order is not "new" at all. In fact, it harkens back at least five millennia to Babel, the very cradle of civilization. And, again, based on historical evidence, pursuing this "Counterfeit Kingdom" never bodes well for mankind because "The Counterfeit Kingdom" is the mechanism by which the kingdom of the world is brought to a powerful position of unity, strong enough to launch another assault against the kingdom of God. Let's call it Babel II. Babel II, unlike Babel I, will be the beginning of the end for this satanically controlled kingdom of the world.

Please allow me to expand a bit on the concept of "The Counterfeit Kingdom" as a mechanism.

Socialism's concepts have permeated the whole earth and are rooted in the great lie that man and his governance can bring life and healing to the earth and its people. All nations are asked and ultimately will be forcibly required to join this

"New World Order.". There will be no need for God or his legal and moral restraints because man's government will provide all you need. (You might want to talk to the people of China, Russia, Europe, South America, Australia, and Canada before joining this new order.) So, lest we lose hope, let me offer you a better alternative, the kingdom of God.

Like "The Counterfeit Kingdom," there is a mechanism whereby the kingdom of God is realized. That mechanism is the Millennial Kingdom.

CHAPTER 9

THE MILLENNIAL KINGDOM VS. THE COUNTERFEIT KINGDOM

Understanding the concepts presented in this chapter is paramount for those who see themselves as members of the church and see themselves as a functional part of Messiah (church). For those who do not see themselves as part of the church, there is still a wealth of understanding to be gained in preparation for the difficult days ahead.

In these times of great deception, it is critical to be able to recognize the characteristics of the kingdom of God. There exists no clearer description of the kingdom of God than in the teachings of Jesus of Nazareth. (The kingdom of God and the kingdom of Heaven are synonymous in His teachings.)

Please refer to the Gospel of Matthew for the complete record. For our purposes, we will look at some key points:

- "...Jesus began to preach and say, repent, for the Kingdom of Heaven is at Hand," Matt. 4:17.
  This is the message Jesus began to preach immediately after His baptism, infilling of the Holy Spirit and His victory over temptation.
  In Matt. 4:23, Jesus continued to reveal more aspects of the kingdom of God as He taught and ministered around the Sea of Galilee.
- In Matt. 5, 6, and 7, the Sermon on the Mount of Beatitudes provided even clearer insight by defining the actions required to function in the kingdom of God.
- Matt. 5:19b adds gravity to His message: "...Whoever keeps and teaches them, he shall be called great in the kingdom of Heaven."

The process of polarization in mankind is revealed in the following verses.

Matt. 13 "The Kingdom of God is like..."

- A wheat field troubled by weeds (tares) which will ultimately be harvested and the good separated from the bad.
- A dragnet. Again, good separated from bad.
- It grows from a tiny seed to be a large structure.

- Like leaven, though unseen, it spreads throughout the world.
- It is as valuable as a treasure found in a field or a priceless pearl.
- Matt. 18:1-4 outlines proper attitudes. Participants must have child-like humility. In other words, one must not be proud, arrogant or self-reliant.
- Matt. 20:24-28 shows a key attitude. Participants must have the attitude of a servant.

In summary, the kingdom of God is not like the kingdom of the world or "The Counterfeit Kingdom." "The Counterfeit Kingdom" does, however, mimic the kingdom of God, and therein lies the power to deceive.

> "For this reason, God will send upon them a deluding influence so that they will believe what is false," (II Thess. 2:11).

"The Counterfeit Kingdom" offers to its faithful servants virtually the same benefits as the millennial kingdom of God! Shocked? I hope so. Let's try a side-by-side comparison.

The Millennial Kingdom of God	The Counterfeit Kingdom
1. Government - Absolute authority over the whole earth, established by God through Jesus, His church and the nation of Israel	1. Government - Absolute authority over the whole earth, established by man through the United Nations/ New World Order/Satan
2. The nations will be ruled with a rod of iron. Agents of the kingdom of God (Israel and the church) will be sent to national governments to lead them in the way of godly righteousness and truth.	2. The nations will be ruled with an iron fist. Submission to the policies of the "new order" (UN agendas 2021, 2030 and 2050) will be enforced by a new world police.
3. Environmental concerns will be addressed as the nations and the environment come under godly authority (Lion will lie down with a lamb), (the planter will overtake the harvester).	3. Environmental concerns will be addressed as man-made regulations are implemented and enforced. (New green deal, population control, no fossil fuel, redistribution of populations and wealth (think China under chairman Mao Zedong).
4. Human rights issues will be addressed by implementation of God's Law, as laid out in Scripture "…the law will go forth from Zion…".	4. Human rights issues will be addressed by implementation of agendas 21/30/50 , as laid out by the United Nations/New World Order.

We could, perhaps, continue with more examples. However, with these four comparisons, we can clearly see the similarities and differences. The objectives are very similar. Who can argue against order and peace in the whole earth? Who is opposed to protecting our environment, or treating our fellow man with fairness and respect? The answer is self-evident: no one!

All mankind has an innate desire for these things. It is as if the DNA of Adam cries out for the restoration of life as it was in The Garden of Eden. The heart and soul of every human being yearns for these things and then becomes fertile ground for the seeds of deception. This deep yearning (motivated by selfish desires) causes mankind to perceive the socialistic Counterfeit Kingdom as the answer to all the world's problems. Judge for yourself based on the results seen in the nations who have embraced this deceptive kingdom.

As in all things, a choice must be made. Choose the real or choose the counterfeit.

To make a truly informed and wise choice, much debunking of too long-held concepts about the kingdom of God and The Millennial Kingdom is required.

Let's tackle the "big one" first. The "big one" is the concept of "The Rapture". For the Church, the devastating result of embracing this unbiblical, self-oriented position is that millions of believers have been spiritually neutralized and will not participate in the founding of the Millennial kingdom of God.

Why would I make such a harsh statement? Because Jesus made the same statement in a slightly different way "Depart from me...I never knew you." Matthew 7:21-23. Believers must learn to reject unbiblical, self-oriented ideas and concepts if the church is ever to grow into the fullness of Messiah.

So, if The Rapture is not a biblical concept, what does the Bible reveal? Let's try --The Resurrection. The concept of The Resurrection is the key to unlocking the entry into The Millennial Kingdom of God. Who holds the keys to the Kingdom? None other than the "First Fruits" of The Resurrection, Messiah Jesus Himself! Who determines the time for the opening of the entrance? The Holy One of Israel, The God of Creation, the Father of Our Lord Jesus, the Messiah. This brings us to the second concept in need of debunking, the timing of The Rapture/Resurrection.

The theory of "Pre-Tribulation Rapture/Resurrection" was brought into prominence by John Nelson Darby in the 1800s.

As previously mentioned, the concept is totally self-oriented and is designed to provide a false sense of security in the minds of believers and thereby blinds them to the concept of the kingdom of God being established <u>on</u> Earth.

By embracing the concept of pre-tribulation rapture, believers are expecting to be whisked away to a place of eternal heavenly bliss rather than being participants in the establishment of the kingdom of God <u>on</u> planet Earth. The danger to believers is revealed in the parable of the ten virgins. Half of them were not prepared nor were they truly expecting the Bridegroom to return, and therefore, five of them did not even participate in the wedding. Now is the time for the church to prepare.

We will soon explore the proper, biblical concepts, but first, let's take a quick look at the fundamental precepts of "The Pre-Tribulation Rapture/Resurrection."

1. A tremendous sound like a trumpet/shofar blast heralds the return of Jesus from His heavenly abode.
2. All mankind who have confessed Jesus as Savior will be caught-up and transported to a heavenly, unknown destination (The Rapture).

3. God will rain down destruction on the remaining people on the earth (particularly the Jews) as judgement for their rejection of Jesus. This is the "Great Tribulation."

4. Finally, God will establish a New Heaven and Earth.

There are two other views of The Rapture -- the "Mid-Tribulation Rapture" and the "Post-Tribulation Rapture." Although there are a few scriptures, like Zechariah 12, which suggest the possibility of a mid-tribulation event, the references are less than convincing for the author, so let's advance directly to the concept most supported by the Bible, the Post-Tribulation Rapture/Resurrection. Let's try another outline based on the Bible.

(Please fact-check from scripture, not other sources.)

Lest we get all bound up in the defense of or condemnation of one position or another, let's remember why we set out on this search. The objective is to make a clear distinction and choice between the kingdom of God (as revealed by Jesus) and "The Counterfeit Kingdom" (as revealed by Karl Marx, et. al.) Having made the distinction between the two, the best choice can be made. Do not allow politics, human emotion, or fear to unduly influence your choice.

Take a deep breath and join me as we take a dive into God's incredible plan for The Post-Tribulation Rapture/ Resurrection, which will usher in a truly revolutionary age of restoration and peace for all of creation. This "New World Order," established by God, will crush the counterfeit, man-made kingdom, and bring light and life to all nations, and restoration to the earth.

Jesus was clear about the concept of Post-Tribulation Resurrection and His return. He often spoke of both in the gospels, but the most profound and detailed description appears in the Book of Revelation. These details were given to Jesus by His Father, The God of Creation. Jesus then gave the details to the apostle John, with instructions to write them down for all mankind to see. Let's take the plunge.

CHAPTER 10

THE BOOK OF REVELATION

What follows is a chronology of the re-establishment of the kingdom of God on the earth, His real kingdom, not a counterfeit:

Chapter 1 - John is commissioned to write down the Revelation given to Jesus by His Father.

Verse 9 - "I, John, your brother and fellow partaker in the <u>tribulation</u> and Kingdom and perseverance..." Obviously, tribulation (not "The Great Tribulation") was being experienced by John since he was nearly killed, then sent to prison in Patmos.

Verse 19 - "Therefore, write down the things which you have seen, and the things which are, and the things which <u>will take place</u> after these things."

John was instructed to record things which he had seen in his lifetime, things that were taking place at the time of his writing, and the things which would take place in the future.

Chapters 2 and 3 - Jesus identifies strengths and weaknesses in the seven churches in Asia Minor (perhaps a metaphor for seven types of churches) and encourages perseverance in tribulation. He calls them to repentance from unspiritual or unrighteous acts. Perhaps it would be a fruitful exercise for every church to read through these two chapters and determine which of the seven churches reflects its own characteristics.

Chapter 4 - God is honored and worshiped in Heaven. Verse 8 – "Holy, Holy, Holy is the Lord God, The Almighty, Who was and Who is and Who is to come." Verse 11 - "Worthy are You, our Lord and our God, to receive Glory and honor and power; for You created all things, and because of Your will they existed, and were created."

Chapter 5 - Jesus is honored and worshiped in Heaven and earth because He was the only one found worthy to open the sealed book, which would reveal and initiate the process that would establish the Millennial kingdom of God on Earth.

Verses 9 and 10 - "Worthy are You to take the book and to break its seals; for You were slain, and purchased <u>for God,</u> with Your blood, men from every tribe and tongue and people and nation, and You have made them to be a Kingdom and Priests to our God; and they will reign upon the Earth."

Verse 12 - "Worthy is the Lamb that was slain to receive power and riches and wisdom and strength and honor and glory and blessing."

Verse 13 - "And every created thing which is in Heaven and on Earth and under the Earth and on the sea, and all things in them, I heard saying, "to Him who sits on the throne (God), and to the Lamb (Jesus), be blessing and honor and glory and dominion forever and ever."

Chapter 6 - Past, present, and future tribulation on the earth is represented by the loss of peace, ongoing warfare, famine, plagues, and persecution of God's two witnesses (verses 9-11). Verses 12-17 announce the impending Great Tribulation, with full details revealed in chapters 8 and 9.

Chapter 7 - God identifies His two witnesses: Israel, by a mark on their forehead, and the Church, by the white robes made pure by the blood of the Lamb, <u>before</u> the Great

Tribulation. Verse 3 – "Do not harm the Earth or the Sea or the trees <u>until</u> we have sealed the bond-servants of our God on their foreheads."

Verses 13 and 14 - "Then one of the elders asked, 'These who are clothed in white robes, who are they and where have they come from?' I said to him, 'My Lord, you know.' And He said to me, 'These are the ones who <u>come</u> out of the <u>Great Tribulation.</u>'" If we refer to chapter 7:4-9, clearly the reference is to Israel and the Church. These verses solidly establish that the Church and Israel will have gone through the Great Tribulation because the imperfect tense of the verb "come" is used. Why is it so critically important for the Church of today to get this concept right? Because we are rapidly approaching the time of the Great Tribulation, and the Church is expecting to be "Raptured out" before it happens. How can the church fulfill her role in God's restoration process if she is blissfully ignorant of the most fundamental truths revealed in the Bible through the teachings of our Lord Jesus? Wake up, church! "The Counterfeit Kingdom" of the world has lulled you to sleep with sweet teachings of love, prosperity, and false promises.

"The Counterfeit Kingdom" is firmly entrenched around the world and is today being embraced by the U.S.A. The Beast

Government and the False Prophet are forming right before our eyes today! If the church is to fulfill its critical role in this process of redemption, she must wholly abandon (repent from) this false doctrine of Pre-Tribulation Rapture.

Chapters 8 and 9 - The Great Tribulation

We are about to observe the full revelation of <u>The Great Tribulation.</u> The gravity of the situation is revealed in Chapter 8, verse 1: "And when He (Jesus) broke the seventh seal, there was silence in Heaven for about half an hour." All the heavenly host are apparently dumbfounded by the magnitude of what is about to happen, and rightly so. The Great Tribulation is a dreadful event and is ushered in by the sounding of trumpets.

At the blast of the first trumpet, a third of Earth's plants are burned and destroyed.

At the blast of the second trumpet, a third of the sea, a third of sea life, and a third of the world's ships are destroyed.

At the sound of the third trumpet, a third of Earth's fresh water is contaminated and unusable.

At the sound of the fourth trumpet, the amount of life sustaining light is reduced by one third.

At the sound of the fifth trumpet, fearsome creatures are released to torment mankind for five months. Only men with God's identifying mark are spared. At the sound of the sixth trumpet, a two hundred-million-man army destroys one third of mankind. The current world population is approximately 8 billion. That computes to more than 2.5 billion lives lost. It sounds like a Great Tribulation period and dwarfs all previous war casualties.

The seventh trumpet is about to be sounded, but first ...

Chapter 10 - All prophecy is fulfilled, and God announces there will be no more delay in sending Jesus to establish God's kingdom on Earth.

Verses 5 and 6 - "And the angel whom I saw standing on the sea and on the land lifted up his right hand to Heaven, and swore by Him Who lives forever and ever, who created Heaven and the things in it, and the Earth and the things in it, and the sea and the things in it, <u>that there shall be delay no longer.</u>"

Verse 7 - "But in the days of the seventh angel, when he is about to sound, then the mystery of God is finished, as He preached to His servants the prophets."

Chapter 11 - The testimony of God's two witnesses (Israel and the Church) is complete, and the seventh trumpet heralds the beginning of the Millennial Kingdom.

Verse 15 - "And the seventh angel sounded; and there arose loud voices in Heaven saying: 'The Kingdom of this World has become The Kingdom of our Lord and His Messiah, and He will reign forever and ever.'"

Chapter 12-18 - Historical review of God's two witnesses and more detailed information of the coming Great Tribulation.

Chapter 12:4 - The Red Dragon, Satan, attempts to destroy the Messiah as He is given birth by Israel, much like He did with Moses in Egypt.

Verses 7-17 - Satan is so enraged by his expulsion from the kingdom of God that he tries (unsuccessfully) to destroy God's two witnesses. (It is worth noting that verse 17 confirms the church as the offspring of Israel:) "So the dragon was enraged with the woman (Israel) and went off to make war with the rest of her children, who keep the commandments of God <u>and</u> hold the testimony of Jesus."

Chapter 13 - The "New World Order" is revealed, as the beast which will govern all the nations, and the religious beast, which will unify all world religions in order to validate the beastly government.

Chapter 14 - A warning to the nations to fear and worship God because He is about to judge the world economic system (Babylon) and release His wrath on those who continue to serve the beast and false prophet (The New World Order and the Unified Religious Order).

Chapter 15 - Heaven rejoices as they see the last seven expressions of God's wrath poured out on the Earth. 15:1 reads, "And I saw another sign in Heaven, great and marvelous, seven angels who had seven plagues which are the <u>last</u>, because <u>in them the wrath of God is finished</u>."

Chapter 16 - Unrepentant man and "The Counterfeit Kingdom" suffer the wrath of God...through malignant sores, death of everything in the sea, destruction of fresh water supplies, fierce heat from an intense solar phenomenon, and in preparation for the attack of a massive army from the nations, the river Euphrates goes dry. Finally, a cataclysmic geological upheaval occurs, destroying the cities of the nations. Apparently, all these events trigger the final destruction of the world economic structure (Babylon, the Great Harlot) and ultimately the return of Messiah Jesus.

Chapter 17 - The announcement of the coming destruction of Babylon.

Chapter 18 - The rulers of the world are devastated by the sudden collapse of Babylon. Verse19 reads, "And they threw dust on their heads and were crying out, weeping and mourning saying, woe, woe, the great city in which all who had ships at sea became rich by her wealth, for in one hour she has been laid waste!" (Remember what happened in 2020? The whole economic engine of the world was shut down in one day by the fear of Covid 19).

Heaven rejoices over her destruction and declares the reason for such severe judgement. Verse 24 reads, "And in her was found the blood of prophets and saints and of <u>all who have been slain on the Earth</u>." What an indictment! This world economic system is responsible for wars and the murder of countless millions throughout the ages.

Chapter 19 - Heavenly rejoicing continues as preparations for the marriage between Messiah Jesus and His bride, the Church, is announced. But before the wedding takes place, the Groom must take care of some serious business: Armageddon! Verse 15 reads, "And from His mouth comes a sharp sword, so that with it He might strike down the nations; and He will rule them with a rod of iron; and He treads the winepress of the fierce wrath of God, the Almighty..."

The first item of business is to gather the spiritual remnants of the "Beast" governments, and the False Prophet who promoted it, and throw them into God's garbage pit, "The Lake of Fire." Item two: Dispatch the massive army from all the nations who were drawn into the valley of judgement. Item three: Bind and neutralize the ancient serpent for a thousand years, so that "he should not deceive the nations any longer, until the thousand years (Millennial Kingdom) were completed," (Rev. 20:3).

Chapter 20 - After Satan is bound, the judgement of those who died because of their testimony of Jesus are judged, resurrected, and rule with the Messiah for a thousand years (verse 4). Verse 5 proclaims, "The rest of the dead did not come to life until the thousand years were completed. This is the First Resurrection." (This "first resurrection" refers to those who had perished because of their testimony of Jesus.)

After living under God's authority for a thousand years, the seemingly indestructible, rebellious nature of mankind explodes as soon as Satan is released upon the Earth again. This is mankind's last hurrah. Their fatal mistake is gathering (once again) to destroy God's Holy City and His government. This is the Battle of Gog and Magog, perhaps the shortest battle in the history of the world. Verse 9 reads, "And they came up on the broad plain of the Earth and surrounded the camp of the saints and the beloved city. And <u>fire came down from Heaven and devoured them.</u>" And now the entity who started this whole mess gets his just desserts. Verse 10 says, "And the devil who deceived them was thrown into the lake of fire and brimstone, where the beast and the false prophet are also; and they will be tormented day and night, forever and ever." The judgement continues.

All the dead are resurrected to stand before the Great White Throne of God. The great and the small are all there: those who died at sea and all those who died who were not a part of the body of Messiah are judged based on God's record books of the deeds of their lives. Death was cast into the lake of fire (no more death), and even Hades (the place where the dead bodies reside) was cast into the lake of fire, and finally, every soul whose deeds did not qualify them for the Book of Life suffered the same fate. (The list of disqualifying characteristics appears in verse 8: "But for the cowardly and unbelieving and abominable and murderers and immoral persons and sorcerers and idolaters and all liars, their part will be in the lake that burns with fire and brimstone, which is the second death.")

God seems harsh, you say. Allow me to recount the record of God's grace. For seven thousand years, He gave mankind opportunities for redemption. He gave us His Torah (teachings). He gave us His Son as His Living Word, and a blood covering for our sin. He restored His creation and allowed mankind to live under His righteousness, His law and His peace for a thousand years. He removed the source of deception during those thousand years. What more could He do?

Chapter 21 - The true "New World Order" is established in verses 3 and 4, and the identity and the glorious beauty of Messiah's Bride (His wife) is revealed in verses 9-27, as the New Jerusalem comes down from the heavenly realm to planet Earth.

Chapter 22 - The end of the curse is revealed in verses 3-5: "There will no longer be any curse; and the throne of God and of the Lamb will be in it, and His bondservants will serve Him; they will see His face, and His name will be on their foreheads. And there will no longer be any night; and they will not have need of the light of a lamp nor the light of the sun, because the Lord God will illumine them; and they will reign forever and ever." Jesus's final admonition to His church is revealed in verse 16: "I, Jesus, have sent my angels to testify to you these things <u>for</u> the Churches. I am the root and the offspring of David (identifying with Israel), the bright morning star." Jesus is the star that welcomes a new age of existence, an eternal existence, with the Creator of all things.

It is highly recommended, faithful reader, that you do a careful reading of the Book of Revelation to garner more valuable insight into the priceless information available in this most powerful book. The time in which we live demands a clear understanding of this book because its revelations are being played out daily before our eyes.

Don't allow the sometimes-bizarre pictures of horned beasts, dragons, and demonic creatures to confuse or frighten you. Modern film stories, video games, and other media constantly bombard our brains with these things without causing undue consternation, so why should we not believe and deal with these truths revealed to the church by Jesus? Be strong, courageous, and diligent to study and fortify your soul with the righteous teachings of the Bible. As you study, understanding a couple of key concepts may help. I know they have helped me.

First, understanding the term "Beast" has been invaluable. In a biblical context, "Beast" most often is used to describe governmental structures built by men under Satan's influence. If one takes even the most rudimentary review of the governments of the world (as you now have), it is evident that the results of man's government, under Satan's deception, bring hardship, suffering, and death to mankind (and Earth). Like a dangerous wild beast, governments of men are destructive and deadly. God has known this from the beginning and that is why He has worked to establish a righteous government based on His Law. The sin of mankind has been so gross that all things in Heaven and earth must be reordered and made new to purge Heaven and earth of rebellion.

CHAPTER 11

THE CHALLENGE

W e started this search/journey to identify "The Counterfeit Kingdom." After successfully identifying it, we have seen a side-by-side comparison to the kingdom of God and clearly distinguished between the two.

At this point, we each have a critical choice to make, especially as the world transitions from multiple independent nations to a single, unified, New World Order. We can join and support the current world movement as it rushes toward the counterfeit one-world government under the control of morally corrupt mankind (Satan's puppets), or join and support the movement to work towards the establishment of the righteous kingdom of God, led by Jesus, and a nation of priests who have been "born from above," and have experienced the grace, the love, the peace, the righteousness, and the joy of living under the authority of God and His two anointed witnesses (Israel and the church, see Micah, chapter 5). The kingdom of God seems to be a much more attractive choice.

The choice before us is simple. Choose life under the unrelenting tyranny and control of mankind, with the accompanying suffering, war, deprivation, and evil, or choose righteousness, peace, and joy under the control of a merciful and loving God.

If you, dear reader, need help with your personal decision, or have difficulties with any of the seemingly radical views and concepts presented in this book, please feel free to contact the author on the web at ldorcik14@gmail.com. May the God of Creation bring light and understanding to you through His Holy Spirit who leads all men to truth.

"CHOOSE THIS DAY WHOM YOU WILL SERVE."

SOURCES

Google search
Wikipedia
Bible, New Inductive Study